If Not Democracy

Essays on the Canton Movement

Dwight Johnson

minuscule media

GovernmentByContract.com

ISBN: 1466384514
ISBN-13: 978-1466384514

DEDICATION

To Dad, who taught me (among other things) why ownership makes a difference. And to Mom, whose wit inspired the name of the publisher, minuscule media. Also, to my wife, Theresa, who, as Traddles said so often, is "the dearest girl".

CONTENTS

Introduction

Representative democracy has failed because the "representatives" no longer represent the people who elected them, but rather themselves (the political elite) and the lobbyists and the businesses those lobbyists quite successfully represent (the economic elite). The means of selecting representatives (majority vote) and the artificial constraints that limit elections to two (and only two) parties result in the reality that even those who voted for a particular representative feel that they only partially represent their real principles and values. Finally, the way that revenues become expenditures takes place within an environment in which the economic problem called the "tragedy of the commons" exists. The economic situation of fiat money, and the impunity that exists for politicians to promise and not deliver, results in government programs that favor special interests, not the general interests, and certainly not the particular interests of the taxpayers who are nevertheless constrained to fund it all.

"Many forms of Government have been tried and will be tried in this world of sin and woe. No one pretends that democracy is perfect or all-wise. Indeed, it has been said that democracy is the worst form of government except all those other forms that have been tried from time to time." - Winston Churchill

Sir Winston may very well have been right about this. The good news is that perhaps not all forms have yet been tried. The elites will certainly be careful not to let any form be tried that does not allow them to remain firmly in control of the people. But the history of humanity has shown a progression, where every now and then the truth of the rights and dignity of human persons is broadly acknowledged, and even acted on. The writing of the Declaration of Independence certainly was one of the most important of these occasions. Now that our civilization totters toward the brink of self-destruction, it is time again to remember these words and act on them.

If not democracy ... what? This booklet tries to describe a form of government of which there is no modern example. It is firmly founded on the recognition of the natural rights and dignity of every human person, and the conviction that government is just one part of human society, perhaps not the most important part. It recognizes the central place money has in the exercise of each person's free will. It proposes a natural form of government where every person votes, not with a ballot, but with his own money. It asserts that if government has any role in human society, it will be discovered by the interaction of persons expressing their wills thru agents whom they have chosen based on the principles and values they share.

The Road From Serfdom

We hold these truths to be self-evident
that all men are created equal
that they are endowed by their Creator with
certain unalienable rights
that among these are life, liberty and the pursuit of happiness.
That to secure these rights
governments are instituted among men
deriving their just powers from the consent of the governed.
That whenever any form of government
becomes destructive to these ends
it is the right of the people to alter or to abolish it
and to institute new government
laying its foundation on such principles
and organizing its powers in such form
as to them shall seem most likely to effect
their safety and happiness.

The Declaration of Independence, Philadelphia, 1776

Are these words of the Declaration of Independence still true? Do the just powers of government come from the consent of the governed, and, if so, how? Do we still have the human right to alter or abolish government, to institute new government? I believe the answer to all these questions is "yes", an emphatic "yes". I am equally certain that the governments we now live under exist with or without our consent, and that we are not as free as we like to think we are.

what a serf is, and why we are all serfs

Not very long ago I came to the uncomfortable conclusion, after a great deal of reflection on these matters, that I am a serf. When I moved to Cherry Hill [New Jersey] a few years ago, I was expected to pay taxes to the township, the public school system, and the fire district. I wasn't invited to, or asked to. As a resident of the township, I was expected to, no questions asked, or else (and the consequences of the "or else" were clearly not pleasant). In return, I was provided services of various types from the town and the fire district, and I got to pay for the education of other people's children. Some of these services I was happy to pay for, others I would gladly do without. But, because of where I lived, I had to pay for all of them with my taxes, because someone somewhere said so.

I also got to vote for members of the town council, and to vote on tax increases for the schools and fire district. Not once did anyone I voted for make it to town council. Not once did the vote for school budgets go the way I desired. But, because we live there, we must work to pay the property taxes, some of the highest in the country. This is modern serfdom.

I am speaking to you today as one serf to another.

We are all serfs because we are forced to pay taxes to the government because of where we live. A serf is a kind of slave. Serfdom, as with every form of slavery, is an affront to human dignity; it cannot be allowed to stand.

We cannot fix a problem until we face the problem in all its painful reality. We need to understand that we are not free as long as we are compelled to pay taxes for things we neither need nor desire. Thomas Jefferson said, "To compel a man to subsidize with his taxes the propagation of ideas which he disbelieves and abhors is sinful and tyrannical". We are serfs. We need to admit it to ourselves. Only then can we find a way to end serfdom.

why political action never yields the desired results

So, how do we end serfdom? Is there a political way to stop being a serf? Will voting for the right people help? The short answer is "no".

Politics is all about making friends for yourself with other people's money. Politicians do this in a number of ways. One way is to please a lobbyist representing some important business, either directly by sending business their way, or by creating regulations that will benefit the business by hampering competition, which can be done either by making smaller competitors comply with costly regulations (ones the already large business can better afford due to economies of scale), or by discouraging any new competitors by creating obstacles to startup too great for them to hurdle. If you have believed the lie that big business is against regulation, understand that they welcome the **right** regulation, if it hampers their competition and allows them to create and sell a defective product with impunity. Just think of health insurance, one of the most highly regulated industries, with some of the most flawed products. Do you think they want to open the market up to competition by complete deregulation?

A second way politicians make friends with other people's money is to create new programs which benefit some important voting bloc. Regulation bureaucracies and new programs both increase the cost and size of governments, to the detriment of the taxpayers. When a politician must spend most of his time raising money for his next campaign, and making certain that his base of voters remains with him, the temptation to spend more and more money provided by the taxpayers (both present and, increasingly, future taxpayers in the form of debt) becomes an insurmountable obstacle to any inclination the politician may have to keep government small. He is far more likely to do what all his predecessors did before him: when things get tough, kick the can to the next generation, and hope you are out of office when things become completely unsustainable.

The very nature of politics leads to ever-expanding government, both in the level of oversight of more and more of our activities by government bureaucrats, and higher and higher taxes to pay for all the oversight and the program giveaways. Trying to bring taxes down by electing different people is a formula for ultimate frustration. As Einstein said, "insanity is doing the same thing over and over and expecting different results". We cannot make any real progress in society merely by making the pendulum swing back and forth.

the best form of government works by cooperation, not coercion

We have, to a very great extent, come to believe the lie that we need government to force us to be better people. Without government, so the lie goes, people would not do what is right by their neighbors. So we allow a subset of humanity, politicians, to behave in ways that other ordinary people could not act. We allow them, for example, to take part of our hard-earned money, calling it taxes instead of theft. We make taxpaying a virtue, saying that, when everyone pays his "fair" share, the whole community benefits. We look down on those who grumble about paying their taxes as scofflaws and scoundrels who are without a spirit of solidarity with their fellow citizens and taxpayers.

The truth is that we are better than that. We do not need to be forced to be better people. On the contrary, the use of force in this way turns virtue on its head, and kills both generosity and creativity. Far better than the outright coercion that is the hallmark of government-as-we-know-it, persuasion and, yes, perhaps a little shame, would produce better social results in the long term. If we truly want to move society beyond serfdom, we need to be more tolerant of differences, more respectful of people, more ready to raise rather than lower our expectations, and encourage true generosity and creativity.

We need to understand the human person as it really is, and not as we would wish it to be. We have to understand that when people are forced to do the right thing, they naturally push back, both directly (by aggression against society) and indirectly (by disengagement from society). It is not hard to recognize both of these responses to coercion in society today.

So if we cannot build a healthy society by force, can we really build it by cooperation? If we can create a society where force is limited to restraining those who use force against the persons and property of others, and for the enforcement of contracts, we can use our creativity and the natural inclination to social engagement to build a government based on cooperation rather than coercion.

we will create a new form of government made of two distinct but complementary components

To build a government based on cooperation rather than coercion, we need to split it into two components, one territorial, the other non-territorial. This form of government I call Government By Contract, GBC for short. I will explain shortly where the "contract" comes in. Suffice it to say at the moment that the idea of "contract" coincides with the need for the "consent" of the governed mentioned as the source of just powers in the Declaration of Independence.

The territorial component can be based partly on the departments of government as they currently exist, whose purpose is to supply the people with various useful services.

The second component is non-territorial, and consists of ideologically-cohesive associations of citizens, similar to political parties, but different in their form and purpose. Since the form of government I am recommending here is based to a large extent on one of the oldest continuous governments in the world, the Swiss Confederation, founded in 1291, I have adopted the name of the subsidiary units of the Swiss government, cantons, as the name for the non-territorial units of Government By Contract. Just as the federal government called the United States of America is comprised of 50 states, the government of Switzerland, called the

Swiss Confederation, is comprised of 26 territories called cantons. Although I am borrowing the word canton, cantons in a Government By Contract are non-territorial. Just as with political parties, membership in a GBC canton is voluntary and mutual, which is to say that membership depends both on the desire of the individual household that seeks membership, as well as the willingness of the canton to accept the membership. The agreement of membership is a contract between the member and the canton. This is the contract referred to in the phrase Government By Contract.

How does a GBC canton differ from a political party? They both are non-territorial (that is, they don't claim to represent everyone in the territory). They are both ideologically-based member organizations. The greatest difference lies in their purpose. The purpose of political parties is to get politicians of a certain stripe elected to office. The purpose of a canton is to provide a way for a group of like-minded people, those who share a particular ideology, to express that ideology within a particular territory, providing services of various types to their members both independently of other organizations, but perhaps more importantly, in cooperation with other cantons. It does this primarily by working with other cantons at the same territorial level (national, state, county, municipal) to secure control of the taxes of its members from the relevant agency (the IRS, for example, at the national level in the US).

When cantons of different ideologies agree that together they can pay for certain government services that are consistent with their ideologies, they cooperate in the financing of government departments that they feel can best provide those services. To put it another way, where cantons are in agreement, they cooperate, and when they disagree, they do things on their own. In either case, the members of the cantons pay for only those services that are consistent with their values, and not for services that are contrary to those values.

Such an arrangement opens up a universe of possibilities for cooperation, innovation, creativity, respect for others, and true generosity.

this new form of government can end serfdom

Such an arrangement means the end of serfdom for its participants. This is so because, when each canton determines what government services its members will pay their own money for, the taxes are no longer imposed by the government but are payments for services rendered, as agreed to by the cantons and its members.

it can end politics

By the same means, Government By Contract ends politics and the need for general elections. When you make a purchase of any kind of product or service, do you really care who runs the company that provides it? All you care about is the quality of the goods or services provided, their cost, and how well you were treated. If a canton finds that the government department it is helping to fund does not provide their service in a way that is valuable to its members, it will either seek to bring about changes to that department, or it will find another way to have the required service provided. In the same way, if a household finds that its canton is not performing according to its expectations, it will either find another canton, or seek to make changes within the canton. Unlike the current form of government, your recourse is not limited to infrequent elections, angry letters, or, more often than not, resignation in disgust. In Government By Contract, you "vote" (as it were) with your taxes. And, as we all know, nothing talks like money.

it can end corruption

There are other advantages of Government By Contract. Corruption is endemic to government-as-we-know-it, because it is based on force. As Einstein said, "force always attracts men of low morality", the horrible truth of which he experienced. By changing government from an organization run on coercion rather than cooperation, many of the opportunities for the use of force are eliminated, and the tendency of government to attract men of low morality is diminished.

it can end the culture wars

Then there is the matter of those issues that fall under the category of culture war issues. I would contend that culture war issues are largely about money, such as in the expression, "I don't want my tax dollars to be spent for [fill in the blank]." The quote by Jefferson comes into play here as well, "To compel a man to subsidize with his taxes the propagation of ideas which he disbelieves and abhors is sinful and tyrannical". But when each person belongs to a canton that pays only for government services with which he has no moral qualms, then the issues remain in the realm of morality and outside of politics, in the realm of persuasion and tolerance and not in coercion. Here again we need to create a society where force is limited to restraining those who use force against the persons and property of others. Beyond this is serfdom, where one group imposes its morality on others, a situation that creates endless and unresolvable conflict.

it can improve education

Running schools on the basis of a territorial monopoly has proven to be a cause for concern. With the tail of ever-more-powerful unions wagging more and more government dogs, we have seen increased spending on education with no noticeable return on investment. Instead we have bad teachers driving out good, more and more being spent on administration, less on maintenance and actual classroom education, and parents who are increasingly alienated from the education of their children.

How, then, will grade school education be provided in a Government By Contract? It is most likely that each GBC canton (I am talking now of a canton for a municipality) will want to have control of the education of its children, rather than having a single school system determined solely on the basis of territory. With parents paying schools directly for their children's education, and professional educators running each school, education will flourish, and the value of the school will be determined by those paying for the service. In the current situation of a territorial monopoly of education, parents who now send their children to private schools and must also pay into the public education system, have, of necessity, found ways to deliver quality education at lower cost. This model has shown, for example, that a much smaller administration footprint can still deliver a very good education.

it can actually lower taxes

Most people think some part of their taxes goes toward useful things, and they are generally willing to continue to pay for those services. But most people also strongly suspect, and rightly so, that a certain portion of their taxes are wasted, spent on programs that they neither need nor desire.

The difficulty of getting control over taxes has been largely due to the winner-take-all process by which government-as-we-know-it works. Part of the problem, as we have already seen, is the political dimension, by which the politicians, in their need to maintain a grateful electorate, and even more grateful special interests, in order to secure their re-election, find it hard to resist the creation of more programs and bureaucracies to further their own causes.

When Government By Contract erases the political aspect from government, it also provides the incentive and means to create government departments that provide just the services that people are willing to pay for, and at the price they are willing to pay. When a canton decides to finance a service that it considers necessary, it engages, along with other like-minded cantons, in a negotiation with the government department, to provide the service at an acceptable cost. The cantons may come to the conclusion that the current government department is not able to deliver the needed service in a way that meets their needs, and may seek out other ways to provide the service. In any case, the members of each canton pay for the services they consider necessary, not the ones that others consider necessary. And the canton must either find a way to provide that service at a reasonable cost, or suffer the consequences of a very unhappy membership, even to the point where the canton finds itself no longer viable. Such pressures, completely opposite those found in the current forms of government, can finally produce a system of government where taxes can be reduced. This is called "right-sizing" government.

it can encourage people to be cooperative, generous, compassionate, strong

A society based on coercion engenders negative responses from normal people. They tend to respond with either aggression or disengagement. No normal person likes to be pushed around by another. No normal person likes to have what is theirs taken from them. No normal person believes it makes sense to force other people to do the right thing, so long as they are not directly and maliciously harming another. Yet government-as-we-know-it demonstrates all these negative attributes. It takes your money by force, calling it taxes, and claims to know better than you how to spend it. It assumes the right to make a determination about what you should or should not do almost without limit. It claims that it is doing everything for your own good. It takes the position in your life of father protector, conscience, and disciplinarian. In so doing, it lessens your opportunities to act creatively in society, to solve problems (unless you manage to get yourself elected to office). It stymies responsibility, creativity, generosity, passion, and solidarity, by taking all these things to itself, leaving you with just two tasks: pay and obey.

In short, it turns adults into children, dependent for all things that matter on the government. It turns people into serfs.

By replacing coercion with cooperation, Government By Contract frees the serfs, and lets all people finally grow up. It does this by placing again on the shoulders of all adults the ability to be responsible, creative, generous, passionate, and loyal. By becoming a member of a canton, you make choices for yourself and your family about what is and is not important to you. You determine what is right and what is wrong, according to your own conscience, and act accordingly. You put your money where your mouth is. Being free, you can give generously from the heart to help those whose needs you see, no longer feeling the need to respond with aggression or apathy. You realize that being responsible for yourself is both terrifying and extremely satisfying. You realize that society does not have to be like a mule train, but can be more like a barn-raising.

you can help begin the process of creating this new form of government

To bring about the end of serfdom, we need to start creating cantons in every place, at every level of government. As soon as enough people are ready to throw off the constraints of serfdom in favor of Government By Contract, real political freedom will be achieved. You have nothing to lose but your shackles.

I have a goal: to make our time the last in history where people know what it means to live as a serf.

Government By Contract (GBC)

During the Enlightenment, when the era of absolute monarchs was fading, many great thinkers pondered the basis of government. One of the ideas that took hold and has sustained many forms of government since then is the idea of a social contract by which the people give consent, implicitly, to whatever government they find themselves under. This implicit contract has worked well enough, though it has provided no guarantee that the people would not implicitly consent to tyranny.

Though the Declaration of Independence says that "governments are instituted among men, deriving their just powers from the consent of the governed", in practice this consent is always assumed, as there is no way for an individual at any level of government in the US or elsewhere to give consent to their government except implicitly. Hence, their right as citizens to vote allows them to change the officers of their government, but not its form, and never enables them to excuse themselves from the powers of a government over them even if they do not consent to it. There is simply no mechanism anywhere for explicit consent to government.

We have employed the republican form of government for just over 200 years. Perhaps, after all these years, it is not surprising that it is beginning to unravel a bit at the edges. There are many today, for example, who feel that their voices are increasingly not being heard at all levels of government, but most especially by the federal government. Two recent examples of this show what I mean. Subsequent to the meltdown of the banking industry in 2008, the government proposed an 800 billion dollar bailout of the banks. This was largely opposed by the citizens of the US, yet passed into law. Likewise, though most citizens did not favor the massive expansion of direct government control of healthcare, that too was made law. Today we face a level of joint debt far beyond any we have seen in the past, such that every household is indebted by the actions of the federal government to a figure somewhere above $100,000 by one estimate, over $500,000 by another. This is a figure that exceeds the average net worth of households (under $55,000 for 2009).

Implicit consent has failed us. What is called for, and what I propose here, is a new form of government: government by explicit consent, Government By Contract. Let me illustrate this idea with an example at the level of a municipality.

The contract I speak of would be between each household and a political organization called a canton. The cantons (there could be any number of them) would specify certain principles as part of their contract with members. Households who agreed with those principles would become members of the canton, and fees (as stipulated in the contract) would be collected by their canton. The cantons would jointly work to approve and subsidize the budgets of the various departments of government within the municipality. The contract entered into between the canton and the household would be for a determined period, one or two years. Participation by the canton in the funding of departments would determine the household's right to benefit from their services. Cantons would not be bound to participate in existing government departments, but could find other providers (or none at all) of the services ordinarily provided by a department, either jointly with other like-principled cantons, or on their own.

Politics is all about power, and power comes from money. Part of the money that provides that power comes from taxes and other forms of revenue. But another important source of money that conveys power to legislators and elected government officers comes from lobbyists and other campaign contributors who represent special interests. Campaigns are expensive. Contributions are made in the hope of gaining influence.

By creating governments by contract, taxes flow to government according to the wishes of those providing the money. Any canton that seriously fails to deliver government according to the wishes of its members will soon find that they have no members. Those members will join or create another canton.

The problem of special interest money effecting elections goes away when there are no public elections. Cantons may determine how their officers are selected.

One of the most serious disadvantages of Government By Contract is the death of political entertainment. No more farcical speeches. No more grandstanding or demagogue-ing. No more promises that go unkept with zero consequences. No more government failure without heads rolling (figuratively speaking; I'm not calling for a revisiting of the French Revolution). All that will be left is the serious business of trying to provide services to all the citizens, giving them, finally, their true money's worth.

Many will oppose Government By Contract. The vast majority of those who oppose it will be those who benefit directly from current governments. That would include those currently in office, all those who directly receive benefits from government, and all those who directly benefit from the political games that republican democracy requires (notably journalists and special interests). The timid will oppose it, preferring to keep the devil they know. The unimaginative will oppose it, putting up objections of every kind without giving a moment's thought to try to figure out how it could work. Those who seek to force their ideologies on others will oppose it, since they know that republican democracy will allow them, through the ballot box, to legally take over the whole mechanism of government. Tyrants love republican democracy. If they cannot keep and hold the government, at least they can be in control of everything for some period of time.

Government By Contract is not about ideology; that's what the various cantons are for. GBC is about form, the form of government that can prevent tyranny and give people real and responsive control over their governments.

We get the government we deserve. I would like to think there are enough good and sensible people in the world that would see the advantages of Government By Contract and demand it quickly, enough people who see the disadvantages of Government By Implied Consent (what we have now), and long for it to take its place as an artifact of history. We'll just have to see what kind of people we really are.

Christianity and the State

When Christians are approached by anarchists, or anyone who questions the validity of the State in any way, they usually go first to the passage from the Gospel of Matthew, chapter 22:

15 Then the Pharisees went off and plotted how they might entrap him in speech.
16 They sent their disciples to him, with the Herodians, saying, "Teacher, we know that you are a truthful man and that you teach the way of God in accordance with the truth. And you are not concerned with anyone's opinion, for you do not regard a person's status.
17 Tell us, then, what is your opinion: Is it lawful to pay the census tax to Caesar or not?"
18 Knowing their malice, Jesus said, "Why are you testing me, you hypocrites?
19 Show me the coin that pays the census tax." Then they handed him the Roman coin.
20 He said to them, "Whose image is this and whose inscription?"
21 They replied, "Caesar's." At that he said to them, "Then repay to Caesar what belongs to Caesar and to God what belongs to God."
22 When they heard this they were amazed, and leaving him they went away.

Is this justification for the State, or for taxes? Consider first that the Herodians were trying to entrap Jesus, asking a question in which either answer they expected he might respond with would cause him problems. If he answered that it is NOT lawful to pay the census tax, they could turn him in to the authorities. If he said that it IS lawful to pay the census tax, the crowds who considered him a prophet would turn against him. So he choose not to answer either way that they were expecting.

The answer he gave could be interpreted as an endorsement of property rights: give to Caesar what is Caesar's. Many Christians, for some reason, want the answer he actually gave to in fact be a confirmation of the question in the positive: yes, it IS lawful to pay the census (or any other government) tax. But clearly, if he meant that, he would have said that, unless he simply did not want to have to deal with the issue on their terms and not his own. And so, the question goes unanswered by this particular passage.

Not getting a satisfactorily conclusive answer here, a Christian might then turn to the letter to the Romans, chapter 13:

1 Let every person be subordinate to the higher authorities, for there is no authority except from God, and those that exist have been established by God.
2 Therefore, whoever resists authority opposes what God has appointed, and those who oppose it will bring judgment upon themselves.
3 For rulers are not a cause of fear to good conduct, but to evil. Do you wish to have no fear of authority? Then do what is good and you will receive approval from it,
4 for it is a servant of God for your good. But if you do evil, be afraid, for it does not bear the sword without purpose; it is the servant of God to inflict wrath on the evildoer.
5 Therefore, it is necessary to be subject not only because of the wrath but also because of conscience.
6 This is why you also pay taxes, for the authorities are ministers of God, devoting themselves to this very thing.
7 Pay to all their dues, taxes to whom taxes are due, toll to whom toll is due, respect to whom respect is due, honor to whom honor is due.

Certainly this is clear enough! How could anyone argue with this!? On the face of it, it looks irrefutable, that is, until you check out a couple of other passages, such as this one from the first letter to the Corinthians, chapter 14:

32 Indeed, the spirits of prophets are under the prophets' control,
33 since he is not the God of disorder but of peace. As in all the churches of the holy ones,
34 women should keep silent in the churches, for they are not allowed to speak, but should be subordinate, as even the law says.
35 But if they want to learn anything, they should ask their husbands at home. For it is improper for a woman to speak in the church.

Well, perhaps women's voices should not be heard in the churches, though few today would agree with this. We are told that passages like this are culturally conditioned, and not meant for all times and places.

And what about this passage from the letter to the Ephesians, chapter 6?

5 Slaves, be obedient to your human masters with fear and trembling, in sincerity of heart, as to Christ,
6 not only when being watched, as currying favor, but as slaves of Christ, doing the will of God from the heart,
7 willingly serving the Lord and not human beings,
8 knowing that each will be requited from the Lord for whatever good he does, whether he is slave or free.
9 Masters, act in the same way toward them, and stop bullying, knowing that both they and you have a Master in heaven and that with him there is no partiality.

If you get any people agreeing that women should be silent in church, you will get even fewer who would support slavery. So if slavery is no longer valid, what about the state? Is the passage from Romans also subject to a reinterpretation due to the passage of time and the changes in culture?

To answer this, let's consider how Jesus himself dealt with issues of the state. We've already seen that he did not want to address the issue of taxes directly at the time he was challenged about them. But there is another instance in the Gospels that talks about taxes. In this passage from the Gospel of Matthew, chapter 17, Peter first answers on behalf of Jesus, then gets a deeper lesson from him.

24 When they came to Capernaum, the collectors of the temple tax approached Peter and said, "Doesn't your teacher pay the temple tax?"
25 "Yes," he said. When he came into the house, before he had time to speak, Jesus asked him, "What is your opinion, Simon? From whom do the kings of the earth take tolls or census tax? From their subjects or from foreigners?"
26 When he said, "From foreigners," Jesus said to him, "Then the subjects are exempt.
27 But that we may not offend them, go to the sea, drop in a hook, and take the first fish that comes up. Open its mouth and you will find a coin worth twice the temple tax. Give that to them for me and for you."

Based on what he says here, it could be assumed that Jesus thought that he and his disciples (at least) should be exempt from paying the temple tax. He chooses to pay the tax so as not to "offend them", and he also chooses to do it, not from what money they may have had on hand, but in an almost comical way. In what might be seen as a punishment for agreeing to pay the tax in the first place, he has Peter go fishing, and extract the coin needed to pay their tax from the mouth of the first fish he manages to catch. Yes, this is certainly a miracle, but if Jesus wanted to pay the tax without making his point with Peter, he could have easily and simply produced the coin in a more direct way.

Finally, throughout the Gospels, Jesus is referred to by the masses as the "Son of David", the rightful heir to David's throne and kingship. There were several occasions, in fact, where, when it seemed that the crowds were about to force the kingship on Jesus, he managed to slip away from them.

If Jesus had considered the State to be a useful organization in human society, and if he himself did not want to accept the kingship, could he not have put another in that role, with the roaring approval of the crowds? We often hear the expression "Church and State" and think that there is some meaningful symmetry between the two words, but is there? When Jesus establishes the Church on the shoulders of Saint Peter, he says that "the gates of hell shall not prevail against it". That sounds pretty important. But what does Jesus says about the State? There is certainly no grand saying like "the gates of hell shall not prevail against it". When the subject even comes up, he seems to be evasive about it, not wanting to have to deal with it yet. When given the opportunity to become king (or king-maker), he avoids it. When given the opportunity to speak clearly about the value of taxes, he cleverly avoids a direct answer. Had he considered them of value, might he not have said something like this: "not to the Romans, but there will come a time...", yet we have no guidance along those lines.

What we have instead is a sense that the state, like slavery, is something that we must put up with for now, but that the time will come when the evil institutions in human society will need to be dealt with, and that we will, at the appropriate time, find within ourselves the strength to do so.

The Immorality of Coercion

Some people see government as a positive force in human society. Others see it as a necessary evil, something that has its flaws, but that we need nonetheless. Still others, myself included, see that there is a terrible flaw in government-as-we-know-it, government that is based on coercion.

That terrible and fatal flaw in coercive government comes from the very fact that it operates by coercion, because it is this basis that runs contrary to basic human rights, rights we have by nature and nature's God. In stark contrast to government by coercion is the type of government described by the Declaration of Independence, which recognizes human nature and the inalienable rights that come from it, and the government by consent that naturally follows from those rights.

Any government that does not recognize human nature, and the rights that naturally flow from that nature, is thereby unnatural, and has the seed of its own destruction within it. This would not be so bad if it was only the government that was destroyed by this failure to understand human nature. The great and enduring tragedy, however, is that this fatal flaw in government by coercion results in the destruction of human society to a staggering extent, and the enormous human suffering that comes with it. Failure to properly perceive the flaw in government by coercion results in war, tyranny, and the inevitable destruction of the livelihood of millions of people, if not the direct destruction of the people themselves.

The people who see government by coercion as either beneficial to humanity or no more that a necessary evil look upon the evils that seem to come so easily from the hearts of their fellow men, evils that they see government protecting them from, and fail to recognize how much of this evil comes from a reaction against the inhumanity of government rather than the failings of human nature. When government is based on a proposition that coercion is a necessary and core element of government, that people must, in fact, be forced to do what is right (beyond what is required to protect life and property), it is the government itself that produces in its unhappy subjects violent reactions. It is impossible that government by coercion could fail to produce revulsion and violence in many of the people it oppresses. The human rights written on the hearts of every person will recognize the evil of repression that government inflicts, and will oppose it, consciously or otherwise.

What will save us from this calamity? We need to recognize the flaw that exists in government that does not operate on the basis of free human choice, on the true consent of all governed. We need to create the structures of human cooperation that can replace government by coercion with government by cooperation.

We are so far from this, it seems to me that it might take centuries more of human misery to recognize the truth of the inherent flaw within government by coercion, and to have the courage and conviction it will take to build governments based on cooperation and consent. That would be tragic.

USA vs America

It is understandable that the word "America" is often used interchangeably with "the United States of America", but the two expressions do not describe the same thing. "America" describes the place on the North American continent that many of us call home. "The United States of America" describes a national government that was ratified back in 1788. Before that, America had a confederation form of government which lasted from March 1, 1781 until June 21, 1788, when the State of New Hampshire became the ninth state of the original thirteen to ratify the new constitution. America has thus far had two national governments.

The current national government, the United States of America, has become delusional. It refuses to face the fact that it is deeply in debt, continuing to operate as if nothing is wrong, spending money it doesn't have at a huge rate on disordered military misadventures around the world, as the throbbing empire it has become. The people of America, meanwhile, are beginning to see the reality, as the bracing ice water of a crippled and disintegrating economy puts more and more of us in the grip of personal impoverishment. There is nothing quite like being out of work for over two years while struggling to sustain oneself and one's family without diving into depths of despair to help a person see things as they really are. How much longer can the monster government, the United States of America, survive, dragging the people of America down with it?

If only the simple solution, UN-ratifying the constitution, would fix the problem. Certainly that would go a long way to fixing the problem, since what is left in America is the fifty states. But would all those states, some with multiple nuclear missile silos, play well together? Would they go back to a confederation form of government, or perhaps start over again with the US Constitution? Would the people have learned enough from the current experience to realize that they have been living under an oligarchy that has made them serfs, that any government that imposes taxes on them makes them victims of involuntary servitude?

In short, have we had enough of government by coercion? Are we ready to build governments based instead on cooperation? Are we finally ready to realize the truth spoken so clearly in 1776 that "governments are instituted among men, deriving their just powers from the consent of the governed", a consent that must be personal, real, measurable?

If I thought we knew enough not to make ourselves slaves again of another coercive government, I would not have created this book. But clearly all around us either remain in the delusion that all is well with "the United States of America", or that government by coercion is just fine. I am here to say, "it's not"! Every permutation of government by coercion is a form of slavery and an affront to human dignity.

Why join a canton?

Although the canton movement was spawned by people who desired greater freedom in society, that is not why the majority of people will join cantons.

Most serfs today are happy serfs. They hold on to the illusion that things might be getting better, and soon we will be back to normal. They have a fairly comfortable life, and don't see themselves as oppressed by government, so long as the government appears to provide some services at a cost that does not seem unreasonable.

But all that is about to change. As every level of government becomes more burdened by debt, as people feel the weight of government taxation grow heavier on their shoulders, while government services wither and die, the practical serfs will start to grumble, then complain, then rebel.

Up till now they have sought something for nothing, or next to nothing, from governments, and governments have been happy to play along. When local and state governments start to become bankrupt, the people will still want something for something, but government will only be able (mostly because of the overhang of enormous, expensive pension commitments for public employees made during the fat times) to provide a very little for very much.

"But we have rights!" the people will say with loud indignation. Certainly they have long been told by governments that they do have rights to many things, but that illusion will shortly be unsustainable. We are moving inexorably from good times to bad times, from wealth to want.

When that time comes, and it is not far off, we will not be able to afford the waste inherent in government by coercion. We will not be able to afford politicians creating giveaways for their special list.

At that time, people will join cantons as a way to exercise some control over their lives, a way for them to push back against self-serving governments.

And push back we will. People, through the cantons they belong to, will pay only for those services THEY consider important, and they will pay only what they consider a fair price for those services, and only when the services are provided in such a way as meets their needs. They will do this, not because of deeply held principles about freedom, but because they won't be able to afford anything else. The time to spend lavishly based on the whims of prodigal politicians is coming to an end.

So for now, we organize and wait. Our numbers will probably not grow large overnight. But, given the direction that things are going, the worst things get, the more serfs will seek a way out. Let's get ready to welcome our fellow serfs. They will be joining us very soon.

Need for a detailed plan

Today I got a very interesting email from a fellow by the name of Brad.

I am a businessman, or at least I was in the previous "normal". I have no political experience. This is very interesting. How would I go about defining the concept into a step by step procedure? Obviously starting at consensus, and hopefully ending at cessation of local, state, and even federal taxation for it's members, but the plan must be laid out in detail from start to finish in order to gain consensus.

To which I would respond:

Brad, all good questions. You present me with a challenge I may not be up to, since I myself am not a businessman. I see the need for change. I see why politics cannot effect positive change. I understand why government-by-coercion is demeaning and does violence to human beings. I am putting these things out there, hoping others will recognize their role in fixing the situation.

Here is my high-level step-by-step plan, such as it is.

1) Introduce people to the idea that government by cooperation is better in many ways than government by coercion.
2) Get people to create and join cantons, voluntary associations of people who want to find a real way to reduce their taxes and recover the level of freedom that is their birthright as human beings.
3) Get cantons to band together to exert pressure on governments at every level to allow greater freedom in determining how their taxes are spent, even to the point where they are spent only on those services they need and desire.

I wish I could offer more, but I don't think I have the skills. I don't even know if what I am hoping for is even possible. My hope is that I will be able to reach enough people that some of them will recognize what needs to be done, and can and will do it.

I'm not sure what you mean when you say "starting at consensus". If there is any consensus, I would expect it to be about something very small, such as, that cantons could be a means to finally give people real control over government, and that they would be willing to try it. Other than that, how cantons would evolve over time is something about which I have no clue.

Taxes as slavery

There has been an interesting discussion on the Lew Rockwell site and blog, including Charles Burris and Michael Rozeff, about whether libertarians can accurately be described as tax-abolitionists. Burris starts with his article, "Taxes and Slavery: A Parallel" [1], which he follows with a blog entry [2]. Rozeff then responds with his own blog entry [3]. Burris argues that libertarians are tax-abolitionists, while Rozeff argues from a panarchistic perspective that a person could choose to be taxed, since many people seem perfectly happy with taxation (though I feel rather certain that would change dramatically if it got around that people could opt out!)

I would like to weigh in with the following:

slave = taxed citizen
slaveholder = government

Mike, if you see the parallel Burris is talking about in the above way, panarchy is not contrary to tax-abolition, because acknowledging that ANYONE has the human right to be free from involuntary servitude (taxation) effectively enables ALL people to make that choice for themselves. Once there is the possibility for true consent by every individual, the very definition of tax as involuntary servitude yields to tax as fee-for-service, and the very definition of government as "territorial monopoly of coercion" is no longer accurate. The semantic problem is that we always define taxation as being involuntary, while panarchy changes the definition of the term by restoring the idea that the power of government requires real consent by every individual. Any government that operates with the contractual consent of the governed does not inflict taxes, but operates on a fee-for-service basis. Panarchy is pro-tax-abolition if taxation is defined as involuntary servitude to a monopolistic government. The realization of panarchy would end taxation (involuntary servitude), replacing it with a system of fee-for-service. I don't think you and Burris are really in disagreement about any of this.

[1] http://www.lewrockwell.com/burris/burris16.1.html

[2] http://www.lewrockwell.com/blog/lewrw/archives/73619.html

[3] http://www.lewrockwell.com/blog/lewrw/archives/73690.html

Live interview on KZYX

On Thursday, December 30, 2010, I did a one hour live interview [1] on public radio station KZYX, serving Mendocino County, California. The program was the Thursday Morning Report, hosted by Doug McKenty.

[1] http://governmentbycontract.files.wordpress.com/2011/01/kzyx_thursdaymorningreport_20101230_128kbps.mp3

"Rollback" in our grasp

Thomas Woods' latest book, "Rollback" , is one book I will be buying (this evening) as a real book, and not a Kindle download, because I want to be able to pass it on to others to read. His writing is always excellent, his ideas spot on, his research impeccable. In all his previous writings he has pointed out the master / slave relationship that exists universally between the individual human being and every form of government-as-we-know-it. I don't think we can ultimately change that relationship until we have voluntary organizations like cantons everywhere, but I am all for chipping away at the leviathan whenever and however possible, and by all accounts that is what this book is about.

Back in February 2006 I attended a talk he gave in Deptford, NJ, near my home, and cajoled him into a photo with me.

The power of serfs

The recent events in Egypt that concluded with the toppling of Hosni Mubarak, provided a surprising lesson for me. The lesson began when I watched a video of a young Egyptian woman, Asmaa Mahfouz [1], pleading for people to join her in a protest on January 25th. She was repeating, in so many words, a line that was often used by various candidates during the 2010 congressional elections here in the US: man up. Put another way, she encouraged her fellow victims of Mubarak to come to the square and protest the injustice of life under endless martial law, as was the case for his entire 30 year reign.

Many days after watching this video, the real import began to hit me. It is futile to appeal to government for justice, especially a redress of injustices caused by government. The appeal must be addressed, if one is to have any hope for redress, to all one's fellow victims of injustice. Or, to put it in ways more consistent with other things I have said here, the appeal for justice must be made to, and in the final analysis can only come from, our fellow serfs. The serfs, my fellow serfs, are the only ones who can free me from my slavery to the governments at various levels. It is their collusion and submission to government that perpetuates my slavery, as well as their own. It is their standing up together with me that will eventually end slavery for all of us.

[1] http://www.lewrockwell.com/blog/lewrw/archives/77305.html

Your money?

An article [1] in today's LewRockwell.com by Mark Crovelli speaks of why the Egyptian revolt failed. This line summarizes the reason.

It is not enough to demand elections, and it is not enough to demand freedom. Instead, what is ultimately needed is to cut off the beast's funding and starve it to death. No dictatorship, junta or even republic in the world can survive if it cannot finance itself.

When a government can take your taxes from you even before it is in your pocket or checking account (tax withholding), it does not need to ask how you think the money should be spent. Don't want the bailout of the big banks? Don't want trillions spent on futile wars ("Terrorism", "Drugs")? Don't want enormous bureaucracies (healthcare) where equally enormous fraud and waste is guaranteed? In a blink the money is spent and gone! It doesn't matter what you want.

The only way to end tyranny like this is to take control of taxes, and that is exactly what cantons are designed to do. Freedom comes when you are able to choose what joint efforts at every territorial level are things you need and desire enough to pay for willingly. Everything else is slavery.

[1] http://www.lewrockwell.com/crovelli/crovelli56.1.html

Simple. Powerful. Impossible.

This is not a new idea. Mike Rozeff [1] and I wrote [2] about it. Pope Benedict XVI [3] refers to it as "fiscal subsidiarity". It intrigues me how easily we could fix everything that is wrong with the US government by this simple means.

The idea is this: put a series of checkboxes on the IRS 1040 forms, allowing every person who submits the form to choose their canton. Let's be generous about this and include any national canton that has at least 100,000 enrolled members. On April 15 or so, tally up the numbers by canton. All revenues not coming from personal income taxes would be apportioned to the cantons in proportion to each canton's percentage of income tax allotments.

Next, put the cantons in charge of dolling out the taxes based on the results of these choices by taxpayers. Congress would have to consult with the cantons when creating the legislation that expropriates funds, to see who was paying for what. Each year, every citizen would consider how well the actions of his canton adhered to his personal values, and would determine which canton got his taxes the following year.

Simple. Powerful. Impossible, of course, because too many special interests would lose out. Only disaster awaits us.

[1] http://www.lewrockwell.com/rozeff/rozeff334.html

[2] http://dwightwrites.blogspot.com/2006/07/non-territorial-free-market-government.html

[3] http://www.vatican.va/holy_father/benedict_xvi/encyclicals/docu9ments/hf_ben-xvi_enc_20090629_caritas-in-veritate_en.html

The Business of Liberty

The most important paragraph in any canton's contract would read something like this:

I, Dwight Johnson, authorize the Coral Canton of America to receive from the Internal Revenue Service all the taxes paid to that agency by me during the tax year of 2011.

By accumulating such documentation of intent to have ones taxes turned over to the canton of one's choosing begins the process by which the serfs will affect their own liberation.

Where are the entrepreneurs willing to begin this process? We need them to start creating cantons at every level of government everywhere. Let them draw up the contract, and begin to sign people up. To make it worth their while, they should charge a reasonable processing fee. This is how the end of serfdom begins.

Serfs rule!

Democratic governments tend to praise democracy. It gives the people the false impression that they have actual power, while all the real power remains with the oligarchical government and big business. All power in government comes ultimately from money, which is why the money flowing to the oligarchy from lobbyists confers so much power to the big businesses that lobby, and the oligarchs who do their bidding. Even though personal income tax provides 33% of the total revenues [1] of the federal government these days, the people actually derive very little power over government thru it. That money, earned by their labors, never reaches either their pockets or their bank accounts, but is "withheld" by their employers, scooped up by the IRS, and is aggregated for whatever the oligarchy sees fit to spend it on. Tax-payers sit and watch from the sidelines as their money is spent. People used to get monarchs chosen for them by heredity, but now anyone can get elected into the oligarchy, though there still remain a limited number of available seats. The power of the monarchs, whether enthroned by heredity or election, especially the power to tax, remains firmly in their grip. The "progress" that democracy represents is largely an illusion.

Human beings deserve better. The people who provide 33% of federal revenues (53% if you include social security taxes) should be getting some bang for their buck. That is what cantons can provide. If the revenue of federal income taxes went to cantons to be spent according to the principles of the people who supplied the money, the people would finally have the clout they deserve. Think of cantons as lobbyists for real people. And all it would take for that to happen is for enough people to say that that is what they want.

[1] http://www.usgovernmentrevenue.com/

With or Without

The American Revolution was fought against England with the motto "No taxation without Representation!" My motto, based on human rights, is slightly different: "no taxation with or without representation!" Government does not have the supra-human right to take by force what belongs to another. This is why it is entirely within the rights of every person to assign their canton the primary responsibility of securing control of the monies taken from them under the guise of taxation.

But even if a person still believes that government does have this right, surely the current situation of extreme abrogation of their fiduciary responsibilities to the people, resulting in massive indebtedness [1] of every person in this country, should lead one to the clear conviction that they have, by their woeful neglect, lost that right.

[1] http://www.usdebtclock.org/

Right-sizing government.

Let's say that the cantons, several of them from every political perspective, actually get control of their federal taxes, and are able to direct how they are spent. Congress continues to make laws and allocate expenditures, but always with the foreknowledge of which cantons can be depended on for which expenditures, when it comes time to cough up the dough.

Let's further say that the current expenditure before the Congress and the cantons has to do with an undeclared war somewhere in the world. Certain cantons have stated that they are willing to contribute to the funding of any conflict that the current Commander-in-Chief declares to be necessary. Other cantons have stated that they will contribute only to wars declared by Congress, or none at all. Will this situation cause the war to be under-funded? Not necessarily. Those cantons that are willing to pay for the war may have more funds to contribute to this cause because they are not paying for some other government programs, thereby making up for any shortfall caused by other cantons not contributing. Likewise, those cantons not willing to pay for the war will thereby have additional funds to contribute to government programs they alone favor.

And what about those government programs no canton wants to fund? Or what about those cantons unwilling to fund any government programs? These situations could be considered a natural form of "stimulus" spending, since these funds would go directly back into the productive economy, creating jobs.

Thus, every person, thru their canton, pays only for those things they believe in, and to the extent they find palatable. This provides the means to finally "right-size" government.

Make politicians tremble!

Clout in government comes from money. Look at how powerful all the big lobbyists are! Yet the real money in government comes from taxpayers. US taxpayers contribute 53% of all revenues to the federal government each year thru income taxes and social security contributions. So how come we have so little clout? It's because all this money goes to the Treasury, where the politicians make all the decisions about how it should be spent. THEY get all the clout from all your taxes. Just doesn't seem fair.

Does it have to be this way? Let's imagine a different world, one where taxpayers have HUGE clout. How could that be?

In this different world, there are cantons, lobbying organizations whose sole purpose it to see that government money is spent as the taxpayers, not the politicians, want. When a taxpayer joins one of the cantons, each based on a particular political ideology that spans the diversity of humanity, they make a deal with the canton: get control of our taxes from the IRS in exchange for an agreement with politicians to cause them no pain at elections.

You see, the worst thing you can do as a lobbyist is to cause a politician pain when he is running for election. The National Rifle Association (NRA) is feared by politicians because it can cause politicians a great deal of pain by selectively opposing them. AIPAC, whose sole purpose is to make politicians kowtow to the Israeli government, does so by putting fear in the hearts of politicians at election time.

Cantons, whose sole purpose is to get control of taxes for its taxpaying members, and thus control runaway government spending, can do so by putting fear in the hearts of politicians who oppose them. It actually doesn't take many members to do this. AIPAC has only 100,000 members. The NRA has almost 4 million.

How many taxpayers are there? Ninety million! Those 90 million taxpayers directly contribute 53% of total revenues to the federal government. How many of them joining cantons would it take to make politicians tremble?

Taxpayer control of tax revenues thru cantons. This is the only way to end the black hole of government spending and debt that is swallowing us alive.

Coward's way out

It used to be fun being a congressman. You were looked up to by most people; you got some nice perks; you got to spend a lot of other people's money, becoming, in the process, a hero in the eyes of those few who benefited from your largess. Those were the good old days. But, alas, those days are gone. Now there is no ready supply of cash to give away. Now it is only about making tough decisions about what cuts to make in a federal budget that is always teetering on the brink of collapse. No wonder so many are cutting their losses and getting out.

The ones who remain will, for the most part, be those who get in it for a quick buck. Being a congressman can still open a lot of doors, making the afterlife of a congressman very rewarding.

But, while in office, they will be faced with the harsh reality that cuts must be made, and every choice will make you enemies. What is a self-serving congressman to do?

The perfect answer is right here. Get someone else to make those tough choices. Cantons are the perfect way out for the cowards in Congress. Let the people who pay the taxes determine what the taxes pay for. Let the cantons take the heat. Perfect!

Last Great Popular Uprising

In the book "Eight Ways to Run the Country" [1], Brian Patrick Mitchell [2] analyses the political terrain in the US and demonstrates that the ideologies that exist in America go beyond Right and Left, Democrat and Republican. He specifies eight points of a political compass, which encompass all ideologies: Communitarian, Progressive, Radical, Individualist, Paleo-Libertarian, Paleo-Conservative, Theo-Conservative, and Neo-Conservative.

Each of these groups represents millions of Americans, millions of taxpayers. Imagine cantons created for each of these ideological groups. Imagine millions of taxpayers signing on with these cantons, based on what, if anything, they would be willing to have their taxes pay for, and authorizing their canton to secure their taxes from the IRS. These cantons would then work with the various departments of government directly to see which programs of each department would get paid for, and which would not. Debt crisis? What debt crisis?

All it would take to do this would be the Last Great Popular Uprising, where the people demand control over their own taxes. Representative government by the two party system has clearly been broken for a long time. We the People need to step up and fix things in a new way.

Let the people who pay the taxes determine what the taxes pay for.

[1] http://www.amazon.com/Eight-Ways-Run-Country-Revealing/dp/0275993582/ref=sr_1_1?s=books&ie=UTF8

[2] http://en.wikipedia.org/wiki/Brian_Patrick_Mitchell

Power in too few hands

What is wrong with government? Essentially the problem is that all the power to spend taxes rests in too few hands.

In Article 1, Section 2 of the US Constitution, it states that there should be no more than 30,000 "Free Persons" per representative.

For the year 1800, then, with a total US population of 5.3 million, one Representative per 30,000 citizens equals about 177 Representatives.

As the population grew, Congress decided that it needed to limit the size of the House of Representatives. In 1910 they decided to set the limit at 435 members. Since the population of the US at that time was about 92.2 million, that meant each member of the House represented approximately 212,000 citizens. By 2010, with the population just below 309 million, each member represented about 710,000 citizens. If Congress had kept the initial 1/30000 ratio, the current number of Representatives would be just over 10,000, which would make taking a roll call vote a bit unwieldy and time-consuming.

But we begin to see the problem: Representatives become more and more powerful, and less and less accountable. Each individual citizen becomes less important to his or her Representative.

As the number of citizens represented grew, the amount of money that Representatives control grew exponentially. For much of the early history of the US, there were no corporate or personal income taxes. The federal government sustained its meager programs on tariffs, that is, taxes on imports. In 1913, though previously an occasional and temporary measure to pay war debts (and as a way to stick it to the rich), the income tax became permanent thru the 16th Amendment. In 1943, over the objections of businessmen everywhere, withholding began. This allowed the federal government to bypass the states and go directly to the citizens for funding, turning things upside down, so that states must get much funding from the federal government. It also meant that the amount of money the federal government could rake in was ENORMOUS compared to what they acquired thru tariffs alone.

With the boom in income came the boom in lobbyists, rushing to Washington to get their piece of the action. And with such a nice small number of Representatives to deal with, having a Congressman or two in your pocket was fairly easy to accomplish.

With all the pressures in place to grow government, it grew! And it did not stop growing when the government outspent revenues. It continued to grow on the borrowing and printing of fresh dollars, so that now our debt is as big as our annual Gross Domestic Product. And except for those darn Tea Party folks, and a few rating agencies, there seems to be little pressure to reverse the trend.

So, what can we do to put pressure on government to shrink back to something more manageable? How can we "right-size" government?

We create cantons that give taxpayers the power to decide how taxes are spent. With canton management entirely dependent on satisfying their taxpaying members, the counter-forces of special interests will finally lose their power to grow government in all the wrong ways.

Real representation

How are cantons better than "representative" government?

Consider how a representative, whether Congressman or County Commissioner or Town Councilman, gets elected. All the eligible voters of the territory who still think that voting matters choose their candidate. The person who gets the most votes wins. Seems eminently fair, doesn't it?

The problem is that all the people who voted for someone other than the winner are really not represented. The person elected represents the principles and ideals of the people who voted for him, but not necessarily those who did not.

For example, in one little town I know, the Town Council consists of 6 members, all of the same party. This is not unusual. In this particular town, this party has a slight majority, with the result that all the council members are voted in by a slight majority from the same party. The slight MINORITY has no representation. Seems eminently unfair, doesn't it?

So, how would cantons change this? Instead of voting, taxpayers in a territory would register with their preferred canton. As each canton has a stated set of principles and ideals, it can be said with some certainty that the canton truly represents the taxpayer as well as can be expected. Since the relationship between a canton and a taxpayer is only for a single year, that provides a lot of feed-back to the canton management about how they are doing. The cantons would be very careful in spending their members' taxes, knowing that, if the taxpayer chooses at the end of the year to switch cantons, there goes the money with him. A canton that mismanages, especially by not respecting the principles and ideals of its members, will soon find it has nothing to manage.

Ownership

It is human nature to care more about what is mine than about what belongs to another. It is partly pride of ownership, partly self-interest in the value of what is owned. If we have paid good money for something, we tend to take care of it so that it lasts, to use it for all it's worth.

What is taken from us in taxes is ours, but once taken, it is not; it becomes the property of some government. The government representatives have a fiduciary responsibility to use it for our best interests, of course, but really it is "other people's money" as far as they are concerned. No one representative in the government controls how my taxes are spent. No one representative becomes its new "owner". Rather, that responsibility is divided up by all the representatives who vote on budgets and allocations of funds. Once taken as taxes, the ownership of those dollars becomes shared, a common resource, as it were. The Tragedy of the Commons [1] then becomes relevant. In this circumstance, each representative seeks to benefit as much as possible from the common resource, using it up as quickly as possible for their own benefit, not necessarily for the benefit of those from whom the resource derived.

This describes the current situation of representative democracy. Legislators, and the special interests they cultivate, get "theirs", without concern for the preferences of those who originally provide the resources (taxpayers). The end result is runaway spending, often accompanied by inflation and debt. Sound familiar?

In the last analysis, therefore, the failure of representative democracy lies in its failure to provide "ownership" of taxes. (I am avoiding for the moment any argument that a government has any right to tax in the first place.)

Can this problem of "ownership" be resolved? Sure, there are lots of ways. A dictatorship comes to mind, where the dictator has sole ownership of everything. That's one solution, but not a good one.

Another, and I would argue, better, solution is the one that is embodied in the idea of cantons as expressed here. Each canton becomes a new "owner" of the taxes taken by the government from its citizens. Unlike representatives in a legislature or town council, the management of the canton knows to a very great extent how the people who have chosen it to be the new "owner" of their money would like that money to be used on their behalf. In addition, the management of the canton has a very great incentive to spend that money according to the wishes of the canton's members.

Representative democracy, where revenues are a common resource of an elite, is a fatally-flawed concept. Cantons, where revenues are owned and managed by people operating on the same principles as the original owners of those revenues, provide the fix.

Government at all levels will never be "right-sized" until taxes are owned, and not treated as a common resource of an elite. Owners understand risk, and work to minimize it. Owners seek value. Owners act responsibly, or they very quickly become "former" owners.

[1] http://en.wikipedia.org/wiki/Tragedy_of_the_commons

I miss my old country

I love my country. I have been to Maine and California, and passed thru many states in-between. I love the people and cultures that thrive here. I love the diversity and the unity that we live in. I love my country.

I hate what my government has become. It makes me sad to see how far we have fallen from our noble beginnings. I hate that we are at war with what seems like everyone else in the world. I hate that the government tortures and murders innocents in my name. I hate that, in order to fly to New England to visit the rest of my family, I have to endure either indecent exposure or inappropriate touching by government thugs. I hate that the taxes I pay are used for things I abhor, and all I can do is whimper about it, since clearly elections have no effect.

I love the Constitution of the United States. It was based on a nascent understanding of natural human rights, and proposed for the second time (the first being Switzerland) a nation that was a federation of strong states, a wonderful example of subsidiarity.

I hate that the Constitution is honored in the breach, given lip-service to, and generally ignored by all those who took oaths to uphold it. Their attempts to change it by making it a "living" document has led only to a government of willfulness and degeneration.

I miss my old country. Will someone please help me get it back? It won't be enough to simply live by the old Constitution, as its many flaws have become obvious. Cantons can make it work again, by putting the power back in the hands of the People.

The world at a crossroad

We are quickly running out of options. For a long time we had enough money to cover all imaginable expenses. We could have a large welfare state, with everyone covered with a nominal income in their old age, and some kind of medical coverage. We could have a large warfare state, with a military budget larger than the next ten largest combined. We had the luxury to spend many billions more on "discretionary" spending.

The days of such abundance are gone for the foreseeable future. The proponents of the welfare and warfare states in Congress are left to snipe at one another, to defend their ideological fortresses, but not to make any progress to a solution, because there is nothing with which to negotiate.

As a result, we are very quickly getting to a crossroad, where the path we take will head in one of two directions. We will either move in the direction of a consolidation of power in the hands of fewer people, even to the point of dictatorship, or we will move in the direction of a broader distribution of power, into more and more hands.

We seem, at this time, to be heading toward the first path, of consolidation of power, and dictatorship. Cantons would move us speedily in the opposite direction, toward a distribution of power back to the people, in whose hands that power rightly resides. Which way will we go? The truth is that the choice will always be in our own hands. Will we shrink in fear and lack of confidence in ourselves, and continue the long path we have been on toward dictatorship, handing over our power to others, to take care of us? Or will we finally find our courage to stand up for ourselves, toss fear aside, and take control of our future together? I know which course I choose. How will YOU choose, fellow serfs?

ABOUT THE AUTHOR

The author has had a career of thirty-plus years in software development, and currently lives with his lovely wife, Theresa, in the pleasant Philadelphia suburb of Cherry Hill, New Jersey, known to countless travelers on the New Jersey Turnpike by its prominent water tower.

www.ingramcontent.com/pod-product-compliance
Lightning Source LLC
Chambersburg PA
CBHW060226290526
45789CB00003B/1437